The Ultimate Guide to Becoming an Expert in Fortnite

BATTLE ROYALE

Robloxia Kid

© Copyright 2018 – All Rights Reserved.

The contents of this book may not be reproduced, duplicated or transmitted without direct written permission from the author. Please note the information contained within this document is for educational and entertainment purposes only.

Contents

1. The Basics: — 1
2. Inventory Management: — 17
3. The Gunplay: — 30
4. The Building: — 55
5. Advanced Tips and Tricks: — 72

1

The Basics:

What is Fortnite Battle Royale?

Fortnite Battle Royale recently took over the whole world by storm, but what exactly is it? Basically, Fortnite Battle Royale, as the name suggests, an entry in the battle royale genre which is available on PC, PS4, Xbox One, Nintendo Switch, iOS and soon on Android. What Battle Royale means is you drop in a huge map, and find guns and medical supplies and survive till you're the last man standing. This is usually reminiscent in games like PUBG and H1Z1, and Fortnite follows the same rules. Let's talk a in little more detail about that.

So, you land on the huge map with various Points of interest, find loot, and kill other players. An interesting mechanic is the storm circle, which is a circle that pops up on the map shortly after you land. It slowly starts closing in with a countdown, and gets smaller every time. This allows players from every side of the map to come close to each other, encouraging battles to decrease the player count, eventually until only one person is standing.

However, the main thing that sets Fortnite Battle Royale apart from other Battle Royale games is it's unique building mechanic, which it carried over from its multiplayer co-op campaign "Save the World". Every structure on the map is breakable, and you can break it to collect materials, which you can use to build walls, floors, roofs and stairs for various purposes and edit them into different shapes for different tactics and plays, whether it is taking the high ground, building cover when you're under fire, or simply building a sniper tower or base for high ground and better viewage of your surroundings.

Now that we know what Fortnite is, let's take a look at the Fortnite map!

The Intricacies of the Fortnite Map:

Fortnite is the only Battle Royale game that currently provides the opportunity of an aggressive playstyle, and because of that, the size of the map is about 4km x 4km. This may sound small compared to the enormous 16km x 16km map of PUBG, but it is huge on its own, and offers plenty of engagements both early game and end game. Let's look at each Point of Interest and discuss them in detail so know which one is best for you!

The Major Locations:

Tilted Towers: Being the most populated place in the entire map, Tilted Towers always attracts about 20% of the entire lobby, meaning you'll have lots of competition. But to compensate for that, the whole place is brimmed with chests and loot, with about 50+ potential spawns. If you make it out of there alive, you deserve to give yourself a cookie.

Retail Row: Called the Tilted Towers prior to the major map update, Retail Row is divided into two parts. One is the household side, and the other is the retail side. Both of these get a fair amount of players, and you get about 30+ chests from the whole location. Not much, but the houses offer generous amounts of ground loot, if you manage to survive it.

Pleasant Park: This location was once better, but was ruined by the map balance changes. Still, it offers plenty of kills and loot if you manage to find a shotgun soon enough. The open nature of the place allows for better build battles, and you can easily push up to Tilted for some more action, plus there's a soccer field, so why are we complaining? Having about 20+ chest spawns, it is a decent spot to land unless the circle doesn't favor you.

Salty Springs: This dense town is home to many long-time players in the game. The place is nostalgic, and offers tons of loot alongside the hefty amounts of enemies. The best point is that it is close to the centre of the map, meaning you won't have to worry about the storm! There are potentially 20+ chests here, and like told earlier, houses give a lot of ground loot.

Dusty Divot: Before Dusty Divot was the campsite it was, it was a Depot with 3 big warehouses. It had practically no loot, but people still landed there in a desperate attempt to farm kills. Dusty Divot practically saved the POI. It still doesn't have a lot of loot, but it is still better than the 2 chests at the previous Dusty. You can easily farm kills there, and can then push to any major POI surrounding it, including Salty Springs, Tilted Towers and Retail Row by taking some hop rocks.

The less-populated POIs:

Loot Lake: Loot Lake is another victim of constant balance changes, and is now a place where a maximum of 5 people land. The place still has potentially 15 chest spawns, but the sheer amount of effort and materials it takes to cross the lake outweigh the loot. Still, if you fancy landing there, Try landing in the house at the North, then push up to the Factories at the West, then finally making your way to the house in the middle of the lake.

Greasy Grove: Greasy Grove is a very underrated location to land. Most people only go there if it is the first Point of Interest in the bus' route, however, with about 20+ chest spawns, the location really sets you up with some good loot. If you ever land there, try landing at the Black Top Retail Shop directly in the middle of the POI. The place has a potential of 4 chest spawns, along with 8 ground loot spawns. The restaurant is also a good place to land, but the time to acquire loot there is high as there are 3 floors of the entire place. This location is at the South-East corner of the map, so you have to be really lucky to get the first storm circle there.

Lonely Lodge: Lonely Lodge is really lonely, unless there's a challenge going on there. The location doesn't get the fair amount of traffic it did before the major map update, but the loot there is still pretty good. With the potential of getting more than 15 chests,

Lonely Lodge offers a lot of wood to set you up for early game, and you can easily push West to Retail Row with some good loot! However, the only downside of this place is that it is located in the corner of the map, so if the first circle falls at Tilted Towers, you're doomed!

Tomato Town: Tomato Town isn't a Town, but who are we to say? The place only has a restaurant, a Taco Shop, and a Petrol Pump, with a single house on the side. The loot there is scarce, but the underground tunnel offers some decent amount of loot, about 2 chests and 6 ground spawns. Plus, you can easily push up to wherever you like, including Risky Reels, Anarchy Acres, Wailing Woods or Dusty Divot. It is also close to the middle of the map, so the storm circle isn't a major problem.

Snobby Shores: Snobby Shores comes at par

with Greasy Grove and Salty Springs in terms of loot, but that fact is overshadowed by it being in the distant West corner of the map. The loot is alot, offering about 20+ potential chest spawns, along with tons of ground loot and ammo boxes, but if you aren't lucky, you're up for a long run to the circle!

Junk Junction: This place is nice, offering about 10 chest spawns, but the llama is nicer because it's cute. The circle can mess you up though!

Risky Reels: Risky Reels was a pain when the Week 7 challenges dropped, but it's fairly quiet again. The place offers about 10 chest spawns, but again, the circle is always the problem in POIs located in the corner of the map.

Shifty Shafts: The place totally discourages building and makes bunny hopping shotgun fights the meta, but you still get a lot of chests, ground spawns and ammo boxes. Plus, you can push up to Tilted in less than a minute after you get geared up, so what's bad about that?

The Farms:

Anarchy Acres: Anarchy Acres is a very wide and open POI, and offers the potential of tons of long range fights. You won't get a lot of materials there, but the loot is plentiful, and you can easily farm some mats on your way to Loot Lake or Tomato Town.

Fatal Fields: Fatal fields is almost the same as Anarchy Acres, but is more dense, offering more close-range engagements. Both of the POIs have a Big barn, a Long barn, a house, and small shacks for loot, but in comparison, Fatal Fields offer more materials in its surroundings, while Anarchy Acres offer more loot.

No-one-lands-here POIs:

Haunted Hills: You'll really feel haunted there by the spirit of no loot, because there are almost close to no ground spawns, and if you're lucky, you can get only 5 to 7 chests. The trees there are the worst for farming, and you'll get doomed by the circle.

Wailing Woods: This place is meant for building practice only. With only 4 chest spawns in the maze, you'll get close to no loot, but the place offers tons of wood, so if you're going for that no-kill Victory Royale, you might as well land here!

Moisty Mire: The place is really good, offering about 10 chest spawns in total, and tons of wood (about 100 per tree), but that is overshadowed by the fact that it takes time to traverse, and it doesn't get to be in the circle very often. Still, if you're lucky enough, it is a great spot to set you up for end game in the material department.

Lucky Landing: With close to no material farming potential, Lucky Landing is a wasted oppurtunity. You can get lots of loot there, but with no materials, it's not worth the risk, especially it's in the extreme South of the map and the circle never falls there.

Flush Factory: With very low loot and no farming potential, Flush Factory is a place you should land if you want to build off to spawn island to fail, because that's the only reason why it exists.

How to make the perfect landing to your spot:

Landing in the right spot is key for getting loot first and killing everyone that doesn't have a weapon. For doing that, you'll need to know a quick tip for making a perfect landing on top of your desired building. If you have played a little, you'll know that you dive bomb down to your destination, and at a specific height, you open your glider or umbrella and glide all the way down.

Now the tip is fairly simple. If you open the map, you'll see that there are large squares. Each square has a name, like D3 or E5. Basically, what you want to do is you want to dive bomb one square away so that you open the glider there. For example, if you are landing at a spot that is in the middle of the A2 square, you want to dive bomb in the middle of the A1 or A3 square. What this does is it allows you to glide straight to your destination.

Learning this takes time, but once you get the gist of it, you can glide down easily directly on top of your desired building.

Additional Tips and Tricks for landing and looting

To wrap up the very basics of the game, let's discuss some additional tips and tricks for landing and looting that many professionals and good players use in every match. Let's start!

- Make sure that you land on the ground floors of houses. For places like Salty Springs and Pleasant Park, landing on top of houses is a big NO. Why we are saying that is that most houses have a maximum of one chest spawn and no ground loot. The person that lands on the ground floor gets almost 6 floor spawns and one potential chest spawn. If you get a Silenced SMG out of that chest, you're screwed.

- **Remember the chest locations.** There are about 7 to 8 house models in the entire map, and they are re-used in every major POI. For example, the Red houses of Salty Springs and Pleasant Park are exactly the same. This means that they have the same chest spawn locations as well, so knowing them can save your life in case you are in the search for medical supplies in the storm or want a quick weapon to kill the person in the other room.

- **Always upgrade weapon rarities.** In case you don't know, weapons in Fortnite come in different rarities. Each progressing rarity is better than the previous one, offering better reload times, bullet spread and damage stats. The rarity is assigned to colors, and goes like this. Grey for common, Green for uncommon, Blue for rare, Purple for epic and Golden for legendary. When you kill someone, always make sure to check whether they have better weapons than you, and if they do, change them with your own lower tier weapons.

- **Watch out for traps in houses.** Damage traps got a really big buff in the June 2018 update, as they dish out 150 damage in a single shot, meaning you can get one shot if you are full health and max. Mini shield range. When entering any type of house, make sure to check the sides and top walls of the entrance for traps.

- **Never stay still while landing.** For example, you saw a weapon on the roof of a building and want to go for it. Don't go on top of it and wait for your glider to close by slowly descending down. This makes you extremely vulnerable if you are landing late and everyone has already found a weapon. Instead, spiral down to your weapon and make sure that you are as unpredictable as possible. Not only does this make you prone to damage, but it also increases descent speed, meaning that if you are challenging someone on that gun, you can get it first and finish them off.

<u>2</u>

<u>Inventory Management:</u>

<u>What to prioritize in your inventory:</u>

Fortnite is not like PUBG or Realm Royale where you can carry only two guns and unlimited meds, but goes into a totally different direction by giving you five slots and unlimited ways to fill them up. You can fill all five slots with weapons, healing items, grenades, utility items, everything!

Here is a list of all the items currently in the game during the time of writing:

<u>Assault Rifles:</u>

- Standard Assault Rifle
- Burst Assault Rifle

- FAMAS
- SCAR
- Scoped Assault Rifle
- Thermal Scoped Assault Rifle

Shotguns:

- Pump Action Shotgun
- Tactical Shotgun
- Heavy Shotgun

Snipers:

- Bolt Action Sniper Rifle
- Semi Auto Sniper Rifle
- Hunting Rifle

Explosive Weapons:

- Grenade Launcher
- Rocket Launcher

Fast Fire Weapons:

- Tactical SMG
- Silenced SMG
- LMG
- Minigun

Pistols and Revolvers:

- Pistol
- Silenced Pistol
- Revolver
- Hand Cannon (Deagle)

Throwables:

- Grenades
- C4
- Boogie Bomb
- Impulse Grenades

Consumables:

- Mini Shield
- Big Shield
- Bandages
- Medkit
- Chug Jug

Others: (Items that take no inventory space)

- Traps
- Campfires
- Launchpads

However, we are going to be talking about what you should prioritize in your inventory, meaning what is important and what isn't. Basically, you want your loadout to be like this:

- First slot: Assault Rifle, SMG, Minigun or LMG
- Second slot: Shotgun
- Third Slot: Can be another shotgun for a combo, or Sniper
- Fourth Slot: Explosives or utility items, or Sniper if you choose to keep two shotguns
- Fifth Slot: Healing items

This setup is THE most optimal setup for early, mid and end game. You can substitute the slots of the items, but in general, you should have at least one health or shield consumable, a close range weapon, and a scoped weapon. Now, for some quick questions on what you should prioritize:

Shields vs. Health items:

Should you keep shields (Mini Shields and Big Shields) or health items (Medkits and Bandages)? Well, the answer is quite simple, you should keep shields. Why? Because you already have many items that can easily heal health, such as Campfires and apples, and those are pretty common. Shields, on the other hand, are less common, and not every enemy carries them. You should always prioritize 1 Big Shield or 3 Mini Shields over any amount of Medkits or Bandages.

Chug Jug vs. Other consumables:

This one is a hard question, mostly because the Chug Jug is a very versatile consumable, but it can't be stacked into pairs and is also harder to use in the heat of the battle because of its 15 second consume timer. If you have campfires for extra healing during a fight, you can take the Chug Jug, but do not take it over 4+ mini shields or 2 big shields. They offer more versatility and are easier to consume.

So, that's all you need to know about what you should prioritize or not. Remember, this is just the optimal setup. There are different playstyle substitutions, which we'll get into later on, but for the time being, just know that this isn't a hard and fast setup, you can change it if you want to.

Sniper or Explosives? - The hard question:

This one is definitely a hard question that is asked a lot, and to be completely honest, it has nothing to do with skills and RNG. Let's look in detail at each aspect of this question.

Why you should carry a sniper:

- Snipers are definitely overpowered in the current meta, as they can one shot a person with full shield through a well-timed headshot, which cannot be accomplished by one explosive shot.
- Not only that, but snipers also give you the advantage of shooting a person directly. What we mean by this is during a base battle, explosives aren't that effective as the person can usually build again, but if you try a sniper battle, that may actually result in something, unlike randomly spamming rockets.
- In the recent June 2018 balance update, the devs decided to limit rocket ammo to 12 extra in order to prevent their dominance in end game. This makes them severely underpowered since you can't spam a lot of rockets, which is why you should pick up the sniper.

Why you should carry explosives:

- Weapons like the Rocket Launcher are devastating at close range. Each rocket does 125 damage, which is just about the same as a Legendary Bolt Action sniper body shot.
- The Grenade launcher is really good at demolishing bases, especially if you are at the optimal angle and distance to toss the grenades directly into the enemy base. The fast grenade fire rate makes the Grenade Launcher a very overpowered weapon, so thankfully the developers introduced a limit for carrying rockets.

Are carrying multiple healing items worth it?

Well, this question is a tricky one, but the answer is simple. It depends on a lot of different aspects. Suppose you are in early game, and you only have an Assault Rifle and a Shotgun, why shouldn't you carry two healing items?

Another simple answer to the question is that it depends on the player's playstyle. If you are the aggressive type that pushes everyone, you have no need of a Sniper. You'll only need an Assault Rifle, a Shotgun and an RPG. That leaves two slots open and ready to be used, so obviously you'll carry two healing items like Medkits and Mini/Big Shields.

However, it doesn't always have to be two too. If you are the Play-it-safe type, you'll obviously need a Sniper to scope and finish enemies without them getting close to you, so you can't keep two slots for meds.

It also depends on the situation. Running in the storm and can't afford to lose your mini shields to carry bandages, just drop your sniper or RPG for it. Like said above, the answer can either be Yes or No, and that depends on what scenario you are in.

Basic Inventory loadouts for all

playstyles:

Inventory Loadouts depend on every player's playstyle. Personally, I prefer to play really aggressive and push everyone I see, but still prefer to play passive if it is for the win. So, without leaving any category, we'll talk about all the different types of loadouts for all playstyles and why every weapon and consumable is required in that loadout. Let's start!

The All-rounder Loadout:

- **Slot 1: Assault Rifle or LMG** – You can keep any one of these you'd like, but Assault Rifles are better for killing players while LMGs are better for destroying structures. We personally prefer to keep the LMG until we find a Purple or Golden SCAR.
- **Slot 2: Shotgun** – Absolutely important for close range combat. You can't substitute

it for an SMG because the Shotgun is the only close range weapon that has the ability to one shot someone with 150 health.

- **Slot 3: Sniper** – A scoped weapon is necessary for long range combat, so snipers are key to the Victory Royale!
- **Slot 4: Explosives** – Very useful for flushing out enemies hiding in cover and destroying hostile bases.
- **Slot 5: Healing Items** – Important in case you get into a fight and need some quick health.

The Aggressive Loadout:

- **Slot 1: LMG or Assault Rifle** – We like to keep the LMG as it is devastating close-range, but it depends on your preference.
- **Slot 2: Shotgun** – Like said above, absolutely important for Close Range Combat.
- **Slot 3: RPG or Explosives** – RPGs are

overpowered at close range, giving you splash damage and instant 125 damage if the hit connects.

- **Slot 4: Meds or Extra Shotgun** – If you want to try double pumping or double heavy, you can opt to leave the additional meds.
- **Slot 5: Meds** – Preferably Mini shields, as they are really quick to consume for some extra shield.

The Play-it-Safe Loadout:

- **Slot 1: Assault Rifle** – For destroying players and structures at medium or close range
- **Slot 2: Shotgun** – For killing enemies at close range
- **Slot 3: Sniper** – For scouting far away enemies in your 1x1 base and engaging them for a long range kill.
- **Slot 4: Medkits or Chug Jug** – These will be your health items, and lastly...

- **Slot 5: Mini Shields or Big Shields** – These will be your shield items in case you get into a fight.

3

The Gunplay:

Understanding the basics of Bloom:

We will start the third section of our Comprehensive Beginner's Guide with perhaps the most controversial thing currently present in Fortnite Battle Royale. There are a lot of things one should know about Bloom, so let's look at each question in detail.

What is Bloom?

Bloom is a major part of Fortnite's gunplay system. Basically, all first person shooter games like PUBG, Call of Duty and Counter Strike : Global Offensive have some sort of recoil system for their guns, which increases the skill cap of the player base. The person that knows the recoil patterns of each and every gun has a better chance of survival against one who doesn't, making it important to be skillful to win the game.

However, in order to appeal to the younger audience, Fortnite's gunplay system does not incorporate recoil, but goes the other way around with bloom. What bloom does is that randomly spreads bullets in the total area of the crosshair, meaning that if you have your aim directly on the enemy's head, you have a 50% chance to hit the shot and a 50% chance not to.

Is it good or bad?

Since bloom is a pretty controversial topic, we have to include this question so that you can choose yourself which one the right answer is.

The good side of bloom is that it does not reward long-range Assault Rifle sniping and keeps all the other weapons fixed for different ranges. For example, you can't use a pistol at long-range, nor a Desert Eagle, making them perfect for only medium to short range.

However, the bad side is a whole lot more. Bloom does not encourage players to improve their aim, nor does it set a higher skill cap for players, meaning that a professional player and a newbie at the game both have the same luck for hitting their shots. This eliminates the need to learn the gunplay, due to which most players resort to going for close range fights with the shotgun, rendering medium range combat useless.

Another bad thing is that it increases the RNG aspect of the game. If you have ever seen Fortnite reddit or forums, almost everyone complains that the game is basically RNG at this point. The full form of RNG is "Random Number Generator", meaning that everything is luck based. Guns given from chests count in the RNG aspect of the game. So, bloom plays a large part in the total RNG present in the game. You can hit almost every shot a headshot, or miss every shot you make, even though the reticle is right on the enemy.

How can you overcome bloom?

There is no guaranteed way to overcome bloom since it is so unpredictable, but the game is constantly improving the shooting model, meaning that they are working on reducing the bloom in the game. One of those improvements include First-Shot Accuracy. Basically, your first shot will always be on point with the crosshair, but the downside is that you have to wait a little bit for the crosshair to tighten. The time taken by the crosshair depends on the weapon type, with small-ammo guns being the fastest to heavy-ammo guns being the longest. Maybe the devs will make more options in the game to reduce bloom, but we can only hope…

In-depth analysis of Shotgun mechanics:

Following the most controversial topic in the Fortnite community, our next topic comes second place in controversy, and that is none other than the Shotguns!

What's wrong with them?

You may have seen countless memes and posts about shotgun damage, the infamous 9 damage pump hit and people that claim that the gun purely works on RNG, meaning that whenever you hit a shot, it just generates a random damage number. Well, we're here to solve all that confusion! The theory that we are going to show is different for all three shotguns, so we'll keep it simple and boil it down to the simplest explanation possible.

The Mechanics of the Pump Shotgun:

The Pump Shotgun shoots 10 pellets which are shot in a cone shape, due to which they spread widely on a long range. Each pellet does about 8 damage to the body, meaning that if you hit all 10 pellets, you get the standard 80 body damage. However, if you hit a headshot, the damage is multiplied by two times, meaning that you hit a maximum of 160 damage if all pellets connect.

The range on the shotgun straddles between the Tactical and Heavy Shotgun, here's a short conclusion of how many shots you hit on every range:

- 10 pellets – 0 to 5 meters

- 5 to 9 pellets – 5 to 15 meters
- 1 to 5 pellets – 15 to 30 meters

The Mechanics of the Tactical Shotgun:

The Tactical Shotgun has the same mechanics as the Pump Shotgun. It shoots 10 pellets of 6 damage each, so 10 pellets is equal to 60 body damage. Bump it up a bit on the headshot and you get 120 damage. The range is reduced to compensate for the fast fire speed.

Here's a short conclusion of how many shots you hit on every range:

10 pellets – 0 to 5 meters

5 to 9 pellets – 5 to 10 meters

1 to 5 pellets – 10 to 20 meters

The Mechanics of the Heavy Shotgun:

The Heavy Shotgun has the same mechanics as the Pump Shotgun. It shoots 10 pellets of 9 damage each, so 10 pellets is equal to 90 body damage. Bump it up a lot (2.5x) on the headshot and you get 192 damage. The range is a lot, which is compensated by the medium fire speed.

Here's a short conclusion of how many shots you hit on every range:

- 10 pellets – 0 to 15 meters
- 5 to 9 pellets – 15 to 25 meters
- 1 to 5 pellets – 25 to 40 meters

So, in a nutshell, if you are getting a 16 damage headshot with the Pump shotgun, that's because only one pellet hit the head and the others missed because of bad aim. The system isn't random, but you need to improve your aim if this happens to you all the time.

Pump action Shotgun or Tactical Shotgun – Which one suits you?

Many people say that only professionals use the Pump action Shotgun, and that the Tactical is meant for players who are noobs and can't aim. Well, that's just false information. Both guns are designed for specific playstyles, and that's exactly why we're here to discuss this! Let's look at each aspect in depth to understand the vital differences between each, and then we'll see which one works best for every playstyle:

Both the Tactical Shotgun and Pump Action Shotgun shoot 10 pellets, but let's look at each rarity differently:

Common:

- Tactical Shotgun = 67 damage
- No Common Pump Action Shotgun currently in the game.

Uncommon:

- Tactical Shotgun = 70 damage
- Pump Action Shotgun = 80 damage

Rare:

- Tactical Shotgun = 74 damage
- Pump Action Shotgun = 85 damage

The conclusion is that the pump packs a punch if we talk about damage, and since there is a 2.5x headshot multiplier on the Pump as compared to the 2x headshot multiplier on the Tactical, the gun is extremely harmful in the hands of one that can aim.

However, what's interesting is that the Tactical Shotgun has more damage per second (DPS) stats when compared to the Pump shotgun, due to it's fast fire rate. Let's look at those stats too:

Common:

- Tactical Shotgun = 100.5 DPS
- No Common Pump Action Shotgun currently in the game.

Uncommon:

- Tactical Shotgun = 105 DPS
- Pump Action Shotgun = 63 DPS

Rare:

- Tactical Shotgun = 111 DPS
- Pump Action Shotgun = 66.5 DPS

What this means is that you can dish out more damage than the Tactical Shotgun since it can shoot 1.5 bullets in each second as opposed to the 0.7 bullets per second of the Pump Shotgun.

However what's interesting to know is that the Tactical Shotgun has a higher reload speed than the Pump Action Shotgun. Why is that? Because each magazine of the Pump Action Shotgun has only 5 bullets, due to which it has a reload speed ranging from 4.8 to 4.6, depending on the rarity. The Tactical Shotgun packs more bullets into each magazine, a mighty 8. But it also affects its reload speed, making it 6.3 to 6, depending on the rarity.

So, let's look at how each guns works

for each playstyle:

The Aggressive Playstyle: If you are playing really aggressive, you'll most likely be pushing each and every base and enemy, so you'll don't have the time to aim your shots. So, you can either try double pumping, which is basically an exploit that allows you to shoot two pump shots really fast, or you can use the Tactical Shotgun. The Tac is more forgiving in terms of missed shots because you won't have to wait for a long time like the pump.

The Play-it-safe Playstyle: If you're the one in the base, you'll absolutely need a Pump Shotgun. When someone is rushing you, they're practically defenseless, so you can pump him in the face for some high damage!

The Bush Camper Playstyle: If you're a camper, the Pump is your best bet. Miss the shot, and you're back into the lobby.

Snipers are definitely a hard weapon to master in every game, including PUBG, H1Z1 and Counter Strike : Global Offensive, and it's no different for Fortnite. Being the only guns that can finish the enemy in one hit (if you land a headshot), snipers are really powerful in the right hands, but you'll take a lot of time to master them.

A Comprehensive guide to always hit sniper headshots:

Here, we are talking about Bolt-Action Sniper Rifles and Semi-Auto Sniper Rifles, since they are the only snipers that have a scope, making this section useless for Hunting Rifles. Both of the snipers we talked about above have a scope when you aim down sights, which have 8 lines, 4 big ones and 4 small ones. You'll only need to use the first three lines because the render distance of the game doesn't allow sniper shots longer than 299 meters.

First off, you need to calculate how far

the player is. There is no math involved, just practice! Start by aiming the middle of the crosshair just on top of your target's head and see how many lines (both big and small) fit inside the player model:

- 0 to 50 meters = 8 lines
- 75 meters = 6 to 5 lines
- 100 meters = 4 to 5 lines
- 150 meters = 3 lines
- 200 meters = 2,5 lines
- 250 meters = 2 lines

Here are some images to show what we mean above: https://imgur.com/a/s1YO5Ni (credits to Fortnite Reddit user u/Mistedlol).

So, once you have figured out the distance of the enemy, it's time to aim for his head! If he is standing still, you'll have an easy shot, but if he's moving, you'll have to predict his movement. That comes purely with practice, but for the bullet drop, here is how you should aim:

- 0 to 5 meters = Crosshair directly on the head
- 75 to 100 meters = Aim the first line on the neck
- 100 to 200 meters = Aim the second line on neck
- 200 to 300 meters = Aim he third line on neck

Here are some more images to show what we mean: https://i.imgur.com/gh8Tva3.png (credits to Fortnite Reddit user u/Mistedlol).

However, if the enemy is behind cover, you'll have a hard time hitting him, this is where crouch peeking comes key. Basically, you scope in while crouched behind your stair, and then uncrouch, shoot and then crouch again. Still, you can't find how far the enemy is this way, so here's an image that you can use to determine how far the target is by their structure: https://i.imgur.com/EV3fscV.png (credits to Fortnite Reddit user u/Mistedlol).

Need to hit a headshot on a person peeking behind cover? We got you here too! Here's how you should aim:

- 100 meters = aim first line on the eyes/upper head
- 150 meters = aim second line on the chest or 1.5 lines on the head
- 200 meters = aim second line on the neck
- 250 meters = aim second line on the eyes

You should learn really fast to estimate how far your target is, usually there's no time to start calculating because you don't want to stand in one place without cover.

Bolt Action Sniper vs. Hunting Rifle - Which is better for you?

Look, we had enough of the "It depends on your scenario and playstyle" answer, so let's talk about facts. The Hunting Rifle is ridiculously overpowered in the meta right now. How and why? We'll talk about that in a moment, but let's see the stats for each gun and how it trumps the other in versatility and ease of use.

- The Hunting Rifle has a body shot damage of about 86 to 90, while the Bolt-Action sniper has a damage of 105 to 121 per body shot, meaning that the bolty can one shot a person with no shields while the Hunting Rifle can't.
- The Bolt Action sniper has a scope that allows you to calculate the distance of the target (as discussed above) while the Hunting Rifle doesn't, meaning you'll have to know by practice the distance of the target and how high you have to aim.

However, the main thing that sets the Hunting Rifle on a higher par are two things which are discussed below:

- First thing's first, the Hunting Rifle has about half the reload time of a Bolt Action Sniper, making it a better weapon in most scenarios since you can shoot the enemy faster.
- The reason why the Hunting Rifle is overpowered is its peek shot ability. Since the Hunting Rifle doesn't have a scope, when you aim down sights, the camera goes above the character's shoulder, and you can see behind cover without actually raising your head. When you align your shot, you can stand up, shoot, and then crouch again. Due to the slow update speed of the server, using this trick doesn't even expose your head to the enemy, so he has no chance of shooting you.

First-shot accuracy and damage drop-off in detail:

First-shot accuracy, as supposed by the title, is a mechanic that means that every first shot of your weapon is completely accurate. We talked about bloom and how it affects gunplay, well, this is the temporary solution.

However, to keep it fair for every weapon and prevent Assault Rifle sniping, Damage Dropoff was also added alongside FSA. This means that the amount of damage done by a gun is lowered depending on how far you are shooting. Here are some stats for Damage dropoff for various weapons.

Assault Rifles:

Common Burst Assault Rifle:

- less than 100 meters = 27 damage
- 100 to 150 meters = 24-26 damage
- 150 to 200 meters = 22-24 damage
- more than 200 meters = 20-22 damage

Uncommon Burst Assault Rifle:

- less than 100 meters = 28 damage

- 100 to 150 meters = 25-27 damage
- 150 to 200 meters = 23-25 damage
- more than 200 meters = 21-23 damage

Rare Burst Assault Rifle:

- less than 100 meters = 30 damage
- 100 to 150 meters = 27-29 damage
- 150 to 200 meters = 25-27 damage
- more than 200 meters = 23-25 damage

Common Assault Rifle:

- less than 100 meters = 30 damage
- 100 to 150 meters = 28-26 damage
- 150 to 200 meters = 23-25 damage
- more than 200 meters = 20-22 damage

Uncommon Assault Rifle:

- less than 100 meters = 31 damage
- 100 to 150 meters = 28-30 damage
- 150 to 200 meters = 25-28 damage
- More than 200 meters = 22-25 damage

Rare Assault Rifle:

- less than 100 meters = 33 damage

- 100 to 150 meters = 30-31 damage
- 150 to 200 meters = 27-29 damage
- more than 200 meters = 25-27 damage

Epic SCAR:

- less than 100 meters = 34 damage
- 100 to 150 meters = 31-32 damage
- 150 to 200 meters = 28-30 damage
- more than 200 meters = 27-29 damage

Legendary SCAR:

- less than 100 meters = 35 damage
- 100 to 150 meters = 30-33 damage
- 150 to 200 meters = 27-29 damage
- more than 200 meters = 25-26 damage

The Hand Cannon:

Epic Cannon:

- less than 100 meters = 75 damage
- 100 to 150 meters = 70 damage
- 150 to 200 meters = 63 damage
- more than 200 meters = 52 damage

Legendary Hand Cannon:

- less than 100 meters = 78 damage
- 100 to 150 meters = 73 damage
- 150 to 200 meters = 66 damage
- more than 200 meters = 55 damage

Revolvers:

Common Revolver:

- less than 100 meters = 54 damage
- 100 to 150 meters = 50 damage
- 150 to 200 meters = 39 damage
- more than 200 meters = 25 damage

Uncommon Revolver:

- less than 100 meters = 57 damage
- 100 to 150 meters = 53 damage
- 150 to 200 meters = 42 damage
- more than 200 meters = 27 damage

Rare Revolver:

- less than 100 meters = 60 damage
- 100 to 150 meters = 56 damage

- 150 to 200 meters = 45 damage
- more than 200 meters = 30 damage

Weapons like the Shotguns, Scoped AR, Thermal Scoped AR, Snipers and Rocket and Grenade Launchers have no damage dropoff.

Grenade Launcher vs. Rocket Launcher – Which is better for all situations:

This isn't a tough question at all, but let's look at some of the major interactions of each weapon before jumping onto any conclusions.

Important interactions with the Grenade launcher:

- The Grenade launcher is just a simple launcher that launches regular grenades, each doing 100 damage to the player and 200 damage to structures.
- This means that it takes two grenades to kill a player with full shield.

- In terms of structure damage, it can one shot Wood and Brick walls, and two shot Metal walls.
- Pretty effective for base destruction, but for close range, nope. The grenades take time to detonate, so you have to get the timing and angle right, or the grenades will just bounce off.

Important interactions with the Rocket Launcher:

- The Rocket launcher, like the name suggests, is a launcher that launches rockets, each doing 125 damage to the player and 250 damage to structures.
- This means that it also takes 2 shots to kill a fully-shielded player, and can one shot Wood and Brick walls, along with two shotting Metal walls.
- It explodes as soon as it touches anything, making it really lethal at close range. For destroying bases, however, an RPG is

sluggish because of its slow fire rate and long reload times.

So, which one is better? Taking in account the stats, the Rocket Launcher is better for both close range and base destruction, so you can say that it is a shotgun and grenade launcher combined. You can use it to demolish bases and shoot enemies in the face, plus you can rocket ride with your buddies, so what reason is there to not like it?

4

The Building:

Understanding the Basics of Building:

Building is going to be the fourth section of our Comprehensive Beginner's Fortnite Guide, mostly because of how deep the mechanics are. Fortnite combines building and gunplay into one complete package that is easy to learn, but hard to master.

To be completely honest, the game isn't about the damage you do to your enemies, it's about the high ground you take from them, and that can easily be accomplished by building. Other players know that too, and they try to take the high ground from you as well, which usually results in building battles.

Building battles require tons of practice and skill to master. Basically, the one who takes the high ground during the build battle ultimately wins the fight because the person on the low ground can't aim directly above and the person on the high ground has a clear shot to the head. Because of this nature of the game, building is essential for survival, so let's look at the basics.

You have three materials in the game that you can build from. Wood, Brick and Metal. With these three materials, you can build walls, stairs, floors and roofs. Each piece costs about 10 of the material type you have selected, so if you want to build four walls, you'll need 40 wood, brick or metal to build them. Now let's look at each building piece in detail.

Walls: Walls are your best bet of avoiding incoming fire. Whenever someone shoots you, you can spam walls in all directions to protect yourself from the fire, and hopefully counterpush them with it. Walls also have the most amount of edit options for different tactics, which we can get to later on. Simply put, they are the most versatile building piece in the game.

Floors: Although they aren't as versatile as Walls, floors provide a decent amount of cover from incoming fire underneath you in case you are on the high ground. They are stable, and have a lot of different uses for tactical advantages, which we'll get to later on as well.

Ramps: Being the most versatile building pieces after walls, building stairs is essential. You can use it to scale buildings, push other bases, and set up your own base as well. They have a lot of valid edit options, and the sheer amount of advantages they can provide make them one of the best building pieces in the game.

Roofs: Called Pyramids by many, it doesn't seem like Roofs have much of a use in a game that encourages pushing others, and that's true to a large extent. The only major use it has is putting in on top of a floor for extra protection. But a lot of other professional players are finding different uses for this unique building piece, so maybe you find a meta strat for this, you can share it with us!

That is all for the basics of building. Next up is building edits. They may seem a little hard to understand, but like everything in this guide, it'll come with practice!

All Valid Edits for Building Pieces:

Editing is a key part of Fortnite's building mechanics, so in order to understand this, you'll need to see the way editing works first by jumping in a game and checking out the grid system. This may get a little bit confusing, but here's a little guide to help you:

[x] = Tiles you should select

[=] = Tiles you shouldn't select

Walls:

[x][x][x]
[x][x][=] = Triangle, used for getting out of 1x1s with decent cover on the side
[x][=][=]

[=][=][=]
[x][x][x] = Middle Wall, used for getting out of 1x1s when half of the wall is stuck undergound
[x][x][x]

[x] [x] [x]
[=] [x] [x] = Side Door, used to get out of sticky situations in the old fashioned way
[=] [x] [x]

[x] [x] [x]
[x] [=] [x] = Window, used for peeking enemies with maximum cover
[x] [x] [x]

[x] [x] [x]
[x] [=] [x] = Center Arch, used for making trap towers and to style on enemies
[=] [=] [=]

[x] [x] [x]
[x] [=] [=] = Arch, like the side arch, but just used to exit bases.
[x] [=] [=]

Floors:

[x] [x] = Regular floor
[x] [x]

[x][=] = ¾ Fenced floor
[x][x]

[x][=] = 2/4 Fenced floor
[x][=]

[x][=] = ¼ Fenced floor
[=][=]

Stairs:

This may be a little more confusing then the ones mentioned above, so stay on track. Here's one thing you should know:

[>] = Direction to move the aim to make, in this case, right.

[>][x][>]
[x][x][x] = Full stairs
[>][x][>]

[x][<][x]
[V][=][=] = L Stairs
[x][=][=]

[x] [>] [x]
[^] [=] [V] = U Stairs
[x] [=] [x]

[x] [=] [=]
[^] [=] [=] = Half Stairs
[x] [=] [=]

All these edits can be used in any scenario, so make sure to use them as often as you can!

Wood vs. Brick vs. Metal, which is the best?

Like stated in the previous paragraphs, there are three major materials that you can use for building, namely Wood, Brick and Metal. Each one of these have their own advantages and downsides, so we're going to discuss that and hopefully come to a conclusion to which one is the best. Let's start!

Wood:

- Wood is the most easily obtainable

material in the entire Fortnite map. Every tree, bush and fence gives wood. However, the most efficient way to farm wood is through the Yellow Wood Planks found throughout the world. Each one gives about 60 to 90 wood.

- Although it is easily obtainable, it is also the easiest to destroy. A standard wooden wall has about 190 hp when fully built, with a minimum of 95 HP when freshly built, meaning it can tank only one rocket.
- However, the interesting interaction to know is that when you place a wall down as soon as a shotgun shot is coming, it will tank the shot and still be up. This is not true for Brick and Metal walls as they have less health when immediately placed down.

Brick:

- Brick is a little harder to farm, but are still found in generous amounts around the

map in the form of rocks.
- It straddles between Wood and Steel in terms of usefulness, as it has a minimum health of 84HP and a maximum of 280HP.
- It can also tank only one rocket, and is best for mid-game bases and 1x1s.

Metal:

- The most hardest to obtain, metal can only be farmed through cars and large shipment containers, which don't give much too, about 30 per one 1000HP container, not to mention the fact how much noise it makes while farming.
- It is the weakest when placing down instantly, but is the strongest when completely built, having a large amount of hp, that is, 370HP.
- It is not recommended to be used in base rushing, but is a better alternative when building your own base because it is the only material that can take 2 rocket shots

and still stand with 1HP.

When you're getting shot at, dropping a wooden wall is your go-to option for building fast cover, because it has the highest initial hp, while having by far the fastest building rate as well. This means that rushing someone with stairs should also be done with wood when possible. On the other hand, bases require strong materials and steel walls are obviously the strongest with 400 hp. But if you're under attack, using fresh steel as cover might be the last thing you do. Interestingly enough, initial and maximum hp of bricks is right in the middle, while the building rate basically equates steel. This makes bricks a less valuable resource overall.

So in general, wood is more effective for the first 6.4 seconds compared to bricks and 6.8 seconds compared to steel. Anything after that, bricks and steel become the stronger materials.

What are the best ways to farm materials?

You can farm anything on the Fortnite Map, but that doesn't mean that it is the most effective way to get resources. In this small category, we'll be looking at the most efficient assets on the map that contain the most materials. Let's start!

Wood: The Willow Trees at Moisty Mire, the Yellow Wooden Planks and Pine Trees. The dark trees don't give much wood.

Brick: The Tall and long rocks. The really large ones give very little brick.

Metal: The helicoptor at Dusty Divot, Metal Railings in houses and Cars found all over the world. Shipment containers aren't worth it.

Tactics to take the high ground from the enemy:

Like stated above many times, taking the high ground

is key to winning any engagement, so below are some ways you can retake your lost high ground with ease!

Tactic # 1 : Pushing up with Parallel Stairs:

If you are boxed up directly underneath the enemy, it is the best way to push up. To do this, simply just edit your way out of your box, and make a set of stairs above and below you. When you build about two to three stairs, turn around towards the opponent's side and build a set of walls and stairs. This tactic works extremely well, but stay wary and don't ramp up too far, or the enemy can shoot you down.

Tactic # 2 : Breaking the structure:

This may sound like a cheap move, but breaking the entire building structure can reset the build fight or potentially kill the enemy. To do this, simply go down silently and then break the foundations of the structure. C4 is best for this, but you can use your pickaxe or Minigun as well, but be cautious because these make a lot of noise, so the enemy above can potentially drop down and take a clean shot on you.

Tactic # 3 : Don't let go of the high ground:

If the fight is the other way around, make sure that you retain it. If the enemy is pushing up by the parallel stair method, just build a floor on top of him and on the sides so that he won't get up. You can also edit down in the meantime and take a quick shot until he is guessing what to do in that situation. Basically, never lose your cool using a building battle, because the moment you get confused, that very moment is when you lose the fight.

Additional tips and tricks for building:

This wraps up our fourth section of the guide. Building is an essential part of Fortnite Battle Royale. Remember, Aiming is only half of the battle, real Victory Royale achievers master building too. Below are some additional tips and tricks for building that'll make your life a whole lot easier!

Gather resources along the way. Having 500 wood may seem a whole lot, but you don't know exactly how much you'll burn in one build fight, which is why you should always stay stacked on resources. When you are running in the circle or simply just wandering around waiting for it to close, pull your pickaxe out and farm some materials! Be sure to be as random as possible, never just stand still and farm, because you never know when you can get sniped.

Always use ramps for cover. If you need to cross an open field and you are being watched by enemy players, run in randomized patterns, and throw a ramp or two as you make your way. When running, place ramps in front of you to avoid getting hit by enemy fire. Be erratic, run up and down of ramps, place some walls in the way as well, and you'll reach to the enemy in no time!

Never use walls when dodging bullets in the storm. If you are in the storm and the enemy starts shooting bullets at you, never build a wall. What we mean by that is that walls block your way, and give a really big indicator of where you are to the enemy. Use stairs to push up, as they give you cover while you're running and provide you a quick height advantage.

Learn to build a 1x1 as soon as you can. Building may take a lot of time to master, but you have to know the basics in order to survive. Building a 1x1 is one of the easiest things you can make in the game. Not only does it provide you quick cover, but you can also scale it up to two or three stories and make yourself a nice little fort. Just build a box of walls, and a stair. Repeat until you get to the height you want.

<u>Campfires have a large area of effect.</u> In case you don't know, campfires have a large area of effect, so you can place down one and add a stair on top. The effect will still be the same, and you can heal from beneath the ramp while peeking and shooting the enemy. Pretty effective in situations where you don't have time to medkit up.

5

Advanced Tips and Tricks:

Now that our guide is coming to an end, we hope that you learned something from all this and will incorporate it into your gameplay. Remember, building is just a matter of practice, and anyone can be good in it, so just keep grinding and you'll be better in no time!

However, we can't just end the guide like that, so below are some juicy advanced tips and tricks that will surely help you step up your game in Fortnite Battle Royale!

Tip # 1: Abuse Traps:

Traps are single-handedly one of the fastest ways to kill someone. Whenever you're in a build fight and the enemy is trapped in between your 1x1, just place two traps on opposite sides, and build a stair to protect yourself in case he fires a shotgun. Just wait for a second, and then BAM, he's dead.

If you want to learn more advanced Trap mechanics and tactics, we suggest you check out a few montages of a streamer SypherPK. He is regarded as one the Trap King of Fortnite, and his plays are incredible!

Tip # 2: Never challenge anyone to a gun:

If you're landing on a rooftop with a shotgun and another person is too, don't challenge him to that shotgun. There's a 50% chance you'll get it and a 50% chance you won't, and if you don't, you've just given yourself a quick ticket back to the lobby. Not only does this ruin your stats, but it is also frustrating to deal with, so in a nutshell, never challenge anyone to any gun!

Tip # 3: Rebind your building keys for better building (PC only):

Building with the default keys is very fiddly, and you'll often get confused which Function Key to press during an intense building battle. So, what's the best thing you can do? Rebind your keybinds. Just go into the settings menu, and in the controls category, you can change the keybinds binded for walls, ramps, floors and roofs. Usually people use Q for walls, F for stairs, V for floors and Z for roofs, but you can choose what suits you best.

Tip # 4: Combine launchpads and bounce pads for maximum height gain:

Many people do not know this strategy, but you can use a bounce pad combined with a launchpad to gain more height. Just place a launchpad, build a floor behind it, and build an arch between the two. Place a wall behind another wall parallel to that arch and place a bouncepad. You'll get approximately three times the regular height of a launchpad, so this tip is fairly easy to execute, but really helpful in tough situations.

Tip # 5: Use your pickaxe to loot faster:

Ever had that moment when you kill someone and accidentally drop your Golden SCAR for a grey burst, only to realize after a few minutes that you lost in the storm along with the other loot? We know the feeling, and that's why this tip will help a bunch. When you kill someone and move toward their loot, equip your pickaxe, and spam the pick up button. Why should you spam? Well, ammo and materials may have auto-pickup, but med stacks don't. You'll have to pick the mini shields or bandages yourself, which is where the spamming comes really handy. Plus, you won't pick up any other weapons, so you can say this tip is a life saver!

Tip # 6: Know the building material stats:

This comes purely with practice and memory. When you are building next time, check the health each structure has and remember it. There are some key interactions you have to keep in mind because they can save your life. For example, Wood may be the weakest in the three, but it is the only material in the game that can tank two shotgun shots as soon as it is placed down. Brick and Metal can only take one shot before crippling down, so they won't stand a chance against a double pumper.

Another interesting interaction is that Metal may be the weakest as soon as it is built, but a fully built metal wall can tank two rockets, making it an effective choice for mid-game base builds. All these interactions will slowly start making sense when you delve deeper into the game's mechanics, so like said above, practice and memory is the only way you can learn all this.

That's it for this guide folks! If you like it, feel free to share it with your teammates and keep checking for more quality guides for Fortnite Battle Royale!

CPSIA information can be obtained
at www.ICGtesting.com
Printed in the USA
LVHW01s2019151018
593628LV00002B/2/P